IT'S POSSIBLE!

Build The Marriage You Desire

Christina Hopson-Allen, LPC

BALBOA.PRESS

A DIVISION OF HAY HOUSE

Balboa Press books may be ordered through booksellers or by contacting:

Balboa Press
A Division of Hay House
1663 Liberty Drive
Bloomington, IN 47403
www.balboapress.com
844-682-1282

Because of the dynamic nature of the Internet, any web addresses or links contained in this book may have changed since publication and may no longer be valid. The views expressed in this work are solely those of the author and do not necessarily reflect the views of the publisher, and the publisher hereby disclaims any responsibility for them.

The author of this book does not dispense medical advice or prescribe the use of any technique as a form of treatment for physical, emotional, or medical problems without the advice of a physician, either directly or indirectly. The intent of the author is only to offer information of a general nature to help you in your quest for emotional and spiritual well-being. In the event you use any of the information in this book for yourself, which is your constitutional right, the author and the publisher assume no responsibility for your actions.

Print information available on the last page.

ISBN: 978-1-9822-7672-0 (sc)
ISBN: 978-1-9822-7673-7 (e)

Balboa Press rev. date: 11/18/2021

CONTENTS

INTRODUCTION

When your marriage is falling apart, what do you do?

Should you:

1. try to make it work
2. leave the relationship
3. pretend there is nothing wrong

Let's pause and take a look at these options. You can't "make" anyone do anything; that's their choice, so it likely won't work. It's also likely that, if you are reading this book, you want your marriage to work, so leaving isn't an option. And pretending nothing is wrong is simply irrational. You won't acquire anything but a broken heart.

Luckily, these three choices are not your only options. I'm offering you another option; *get help now*. I know you probably don't want anyone else dabbling in your marriage. You don't think you need anyone to tell you what you already know- your marriage is in distress, and you don't know what to do. So you may not be ready for counseling, and that's okay. However, if you want your marriage to work, it's imperative to educate yourself and try to make adjustments that will turn things around.

If you want change in your marriage, it's a good idea to try learning new skills. If you've been doing the same thing for years and it hasn't worked, it probably won't, and it's time to reevaluate. That's what we are all about: healing and restoring broken marriages. Restoration comes when two hurting people decide to work together as a team with the same goal in mind. When this happens, healing can occur.

You need tools to rebuild a broken marriage. It's not necessary to tear down everything you've built; sometimes, you have to clean out and clean up what you have. Unfortunately, this isn't always a short, simple process. You have to bring in a demolition team to tear down the old and a renovation team to bring in the new. It takes teamwork, and it takes working together to repair, replace, and restore. Your marriage can be a great experience. You just have to work for it!

When you have exhausted all options, it's okay to admit you need help. In fact, you should seek help as soon as things feel unstable, as you would in any other thing. When a house is no longer stable, it develops cracks in the walls, ceiling, and floors, which indicates foundation problems.

Your marriage works the same way. When your foundation is unstable, you will see the cracks: things like unhappiness, loneliness, isolation, poor communication, and resentment.

If there is any shift in your marriage that has an effect on your dynamic and the function of your relationship, by all means get help. After you've come to the realization that your marriage is unstable, you need to do something about it. Take charge of your relationship. Create the marriage you want by building a strong foundation using tools designed to give you support and reinforcement.

Testimonial:

"Marriage hasn't been easy for us. The first 5 years were the most difficult. We learned quickly that dating and marriage were totally different things. The overwhelming responsibilities and expectations as husband and wife made it hard for us to balance our love with our frustrations. We've struggled. We've hurt each other. However, we've also been determined to develop our marriage and stay committed to our dreams… We've been determined to make it no matter what. Our past mistakes will not keep us apart because we know God's plan for our life and His grace has covered us."

Bringing a fresh outlook to your marriage enhances the effectiveness of your relationship skills. These skills are learned- couples don't enter into a marriage knowing how to handle every situation. Unless you had great role models, at some point along the way, you will start to wonder "What did I get myself into?"

Now, I know they told you marriage is 50/50, but I disagree. In my experience, it's more like **100/100.** You should be a whole person coming into it- not half. You shouldn't expect your partner to complete you; they should enhance you and make you better. Your partnership should create synergy, which should contribute to a fulfilling life together.

I'll be the first to tell you it's not handed to you- you have to work for it. And you should try hard not to become so consumed in "you" that you overlook "us." When you do this, you are putting your marriage in a danger zone that will be hard to recover from. "Us" comes first.

Danger zones are setups for failure, and you should be very aware of them. Feeling neglected or alone, having poor communication, or not being "in love" anymore are also examples of danger zones. That's why educating yourself is so important. You need to know the warning signs that indicate your marriage may be headed for trouble, and you need wisdom to make healthy decisions for the future of your relationship with your spouse.

The *Flip My Marriage* experience can help increase your relational skills and provide a blueprint to build a strong, healthy marriage. Some couples are just starting to create a strong foundation for their marriage to build on. Others just need tools to repair broken areas in their marriage following major transitions in life. However, there are also couples who have endured the tests of time and require marriage renovation only to restore the original beauty. Regardless of where you are in your marriage, *Flip My Marriage* wants to increase the value of what you have.

This book is designed to help you enhance your marriage. We will discuss 5 major tools that you can use to help build the marriage you desire. So get the tools, do the work and Flip Your Marriage TODAY!

CHAPTER 1

DETERMINATION- Hang On and Don't Let Go

The strength of your relationship will be tested over time. You will go through tough situations: financial struggles, raising children, deaths of family members, stress on the job. Or perhaps it's experiences of disappointment, distrust, or betrayal. Whatever you're going through, you may not know if you can hold the marriage together (or even if you want to). You take marriage with the good and the bad, the ups and the downs. But when the bad outweighs the good, and the downs keep coming, you start to wonder "Is it worth it?"

You always hear about "commitment" in relationships. But even more important than your commitment is your determination. You have to be _determined_ to stay committed. Marriage requires both of you to be determined to hang on even when it hurts. You find purpose through the pain, and develop the drive to succeed.

It takes determination to give your best and do what it takes to overcome the obstacles. The key is coming together to find a healthy balance that will lead to relationship success. You must be on the same page, focused on the same goal, and unwavering in your commitment to your dreams. And it's okay if one partner has more confidence in the marriage than the other; that happens often in counseling. However, you must be determined to put the past behind you and design the relationship you want in the present moment- together.

When there has been a significant blow to the marriage, sometimes one of you may be stronger than the other. One of you may believe "it's possible," while the other may be doubtful. Nevertheless, if you both want it and you haven't given up, IT'S POSSIBLE! Identify your goals and take action. It takes love, faith, and commitment to your promise "to have and to hold..." Give all you've got to your marriage, and learn how to be the best spouse you can be.

From my experience with couples, I have found five key elements that will help keep your relationship going:

1. **Commitment**- If you're not in this together, there is no way you can truly be happy in your marriage. Without commitment, there are no responsibilities and no guarantees. What I mean by this is that if you don't feel responsible for the outcome, then there is no guarantee that you're going to put in the effort to make it work because you're only partially in. Halfway isn't good enough!

2. **Focus**- Saving your marriage requires focus. By setting goals and finding purpose, you have a foundation. Without focus, you don't have direction or ambition. Why are you married? If you can't answer that question, you're not focused; as a result, it will be hard to succeed.

3. **Self-control**- You must be disciplined and deliberate. Your emotions must be regulated, and you must keep your composure instead of making rash decisions. Without self-control, you may impulsively do things that can hurt your marriage in the long run. You may spend excessively to make yourself feel better, work more hours rather than dealing with issues at home, or vent to others instead of talking directly to your spouse.

4. **Solidarity**- You have to be a unit. You should be on the same page, headed in the same direction. It takes teamwork- and we know there is no "I" in "Team." It's not all about you. There are two individuals in a partnership, and both should be unified in decisions and approach. Without solidarity, you are not in agreement, and there will be disconnection. And two disconnected individuals can't move forward. They will only go in circles and find themselves tired, angry, and bitter.

Positive Thoughts + Positive Actions= Positive Life Experiences

5. **Positive mindset**- Last but not least, you have to think positively. Your mindset determines whether you think "We can do this" or "I'm not sure if we can." You must have forward thinking, which will lead to goal-directed behaviors. Having a positive

core belief system brings confidence. Without a positive mindset, your marriage won't thrive. You will feel stuck and lifeless. You need <u>positive thinking</u> followed by <u>positive action</u> to hold your relationship together. Remember that having a positive mindset without making changes is pointless. Many couples say they want change, but they are extremely negative and stubborn. Negativity does not bring positive change; it brings dissatisfaction and frustration. Don't just think positive, *be* positive. Let your action speak for itself.

So here are a few questions to ask yourself about your marriage:

1. **Are you connected?**
2. **Are you certain?**
3. **Are you confident?**
4. **Are you consistent?**

Connected marriages are strong. You should strive to be emotionally, spiritually, and physically connected with one another. Being on the same page with common goals and a healthy balance of responsibility will go a long way. Another part of connectedness is intimacy, which keeps the relationship fresh- <u>*Not Just Sex.*</u> Now don't get me wrong, sex is GREAT and a very important part of being connected (according to my husband). However, intimacy is greater. And if you don't have intimacy, that means you are definitely disconnected in some area of the relationship. Disconnection is yet another danger zone that often leads to divorce.

Certainty gives the marriage purpose. If you are certain that you want to be with your spouse, then you are making one of the first steps toward fulfillment. You need certainty to develop a strong foundation worth building on.

Confidence brings with it assurance that your marriage is worth fighting for. Once you make the changes needed to be a better spouse, you must be confident that your actions and efforts will transform your marriage and that you will be successful.

Consistency means you engage in deliberate, daily actions that promote the growth and development of your marriage. You have to be consistent. If you have made a mistake and you want to regain your partner's trust, you have to earn that trust through your actions.

You need constant, persistent actions that show you are committed to saving your marriage.

Make sure you don't expect approval or seek acknowledgment of everything you do- just do it! In addition, it's important to make sure that you are doing the *right* things to make your spouse happy.

Take note of things they say. If you pay attention, you will receive hints along the way that tell you what your partner enjoys or what they are missing in the marriage. By fulfilling these needs, you can demonstrate clearly that you are listening and not giving up.

By hanging in there when things get tough, you are demonstrating to your spouse how connected, certain, confident and consistent you are. You can now begin to focus on goals for your future. Stay positive about the direction of your marriage, even though it may seem challenging and overwhelming at times. It will be your determination that will help build success along the way.

CHAPTER 2

COURAGE: Fight for What You Want

You must be bold and fearless to fight for your marriage. When your spouse has hurt you or it feels like things are going wrong, you have to be courageous enough to take on the odds stacked against you. When you are scared it won't work, fearful it's too late, or terrified that they don't love you anymore, then you can't be too afraid to fight for what you want. You have to go after it with everything you've got!

Maybe you've been trying for years to get your marriage on track. You don't know where things went wrong. You don't know how to love each other anymore, or you can't talk without arguing. Just because you don't know how it will turn out doesn't mean you shouldn't try. Courage will help you find a way. It brings confidence in spite of fear. Courage strengthens you to go through the struggle, to push past the pain, and to do what it takes to win. And winning in your marriage is everything.

So you're experiencing significant challenges in your marriage. Maybe you spent all of your time raising the kids, and now that they are gone, you realize you don't have anything in common anymore. It could also be that she works so hard, she doesn't seem to have time for you. Or maybe he spends more time out with friends than with you, and you don't feel like a significant part of his life. Sometimes, marriage hurts. And it's okay to admit it's painful. However, if you love each other, there is always a way for it to work. And in that case, it's not okay to give up.

If you know she is the one that you want to spend the rest of your life with, why would you quit trying? If you know he truly loves you, why would you mistreat him to the point that he wants to leave? Why are you so afraid to say "I'm sorry" or admit you were wrong? Why is it so hard to love again? Maybe it's fear. Loving again may risk rejection. You may have to let go of your pride or let yourself be vulnerable. Maybe you're afraid of the possibility that it may not work. Maybe you feel like you're wasting time. Here is my question: "But what if it does work?" By taking that risk, having the eagerness to try new things, willingness to make mistakes, faith to believe, and boldness to forgive, you can fight for the fulfilling marriage you deserve. Don't let fear keep you from fighting!

Courage is risky. You're taking a chance that it won't work… But if you don't try- it NEVER will…

When you fight for something, there is a 50/50 chance that you may lose. But if you don't fight, there is a 100% chance that you will fail. And I believe you would prefer to know you gave your all and it didn't work, rather than know that you gave up and didn't even try. Not trying is an automatic failure, and you don't want to live with the regret of not putting forth effort to make it work. And when I say "make it work" I don't mean forcing something that isn't meant to be. I mean two people who give, love, share, and commit together. That's making it work. And doing this in the midst of your fears takes courage.

If you're like me, you don't like fights. You don't like conflict, pain, or the idea of losing. But there are some things that are worth fighting for, regardless of the outcome. And I feel that marriage is one of them. When you stood at the altar, you looked into their eyes, and you said "I do." You said "I do," not just to spend your life with someone. You said "I do" not just for the promise of financial stability and emotional support. You also said "I do" to the challenges, the moments of vulnerability, and the frustrations. You said "I do" to the fight to stay together no matter what!

Everyone thinks it's a given that when you get married, you are committed. Yes, that may be true in some sense. But some people are only committed to the idea of marriage, not necessarily its realities. You have to commit to working through problems and going through the tough challenges that marriage brings. Commitment doesn't just mean when it's a happy experience; it's also the pain.

No one gets married to get divorced, but once you say "I do," you enter into a world of complexities that you may not be prepared for. And if you don't have the skills or tools, staying together may be an extremely difficult challenge. It's important to come together and pursue an enjoyable marriage with a partner who supports you and pushes you to be better. You should support and push them the same way.

If you start to feel isolated, neglected, disrespected or even angry, these are signs that something must be done immediately. Don't sit back and think "Oh, this is temporary. I'm sure it will pass." Don't wait to see if things will get better; take action to safeguard your marriage immediately. This is the moment when you have to fight for everything you've worked so hard for. If you recognize that something is wrong and you are unhappy, it's time to fight.

So, what does it mean to fight?

You have to:

F- Forgive
   I- Initiate
      G- Give
         H- Hope
            T- Trust

This process will help you get things back on track.

Let's start with **FORGIVE.** When you are faced with a tough situation, you usually have these three options: 1) change it, 2) accept it, or 3) let it go. If you can't change it, you need to learn how to accept it. If it's unacceptable, then you have to learn to let go. Let go of the stress, the disappointment, and the hurt. Often, this means you have to forgive. Forgive them for being human. Forgive them for their mistakes and their inconsiderate actions. Forgiveness is not for them; IT'S FOR YOU! It allows you to move forward in the knowledge that THEY messed up, NOT YOU. Forgiveness means understanding that despite the motivations behind your spouse's actions, YOU are okay. You don't have to be okay with what they did, but you can be okay because you know that you have the power to make a choice. You can choose to move forward or you can choose to become resentful and bitter.

If you want to fight for your marriage, you have to forgive. If you want to stay married, regardless of what they did, you won't be truly happy until you let go of the past. Now I'm not saying to forget, because if you forget then it can happen again and have the same impact. But it is important to forgive; remove the pain from the offense and simply see it for what it is.

In order to fight, you must also **INITIATE.** This means developing a plan for recovery. You begin to process what has happened or assess the dysfunction in your relationship, and you devise a strategy to overcome the obstacles. Your plan should be designed to strengthen your marriage and protect it from future harm.

For example, in my work as a counselor I had a couple who was going through affair recovery. The wife wanted to forgive, but she didn't know how. Her shock and pain held her hostage, but at the same time she wanted to be free and reconcile with her husband. I helped the couple create a protection plan to help them move forward. Your protection plan should be designed with your goals, values, and relationship needs in mind. It should also include warning signs that could indicate when the marriage is headed for trouble. When you see the warning signs, you have a series of steps to help keep the marriage on track.

Next, you should **GIVE.** This is the tough part: giving unconditionally. It should be unconditional so that you won't continue to pass judgment, hold their actions over their head, or remind them of every mistake they've made when you are angry. Either you love them through their mistakes or you will not be truly happy in your relationship. If you are constantly bringing up the past- you are saying "I love you, *but...*" You can't move forward if you are doing this, because you are actively holding your partner hostage in their own past instead of giving them another chance.

Key Point:

I've told couples in the past that if you're not all in, it probably won't get better. You both have to be fully committed to the process of change. Learn how to give love and receive it when it's given back. Give your time and energy to your spouse. A positive feedback loop can provide momentum and keep things moving forward.

If your marriage is going to work, you have to be all in. And it takes total commitment to fight. Giving simultaneously makes the process meaningful and gives hope. Learn to be empathetic and compassionate toward your spouse. When they are talking, *listen*. Consider their feelings and value them. Give attention, affection and appreciation. Another important element of the fight is **HOPE.** You have to believe it's possible to be happy in your marriage. Belief is powerful. Sometimes it takes blind faith to believe your spouse is genuinely sorry if they have made a mistake. You also have to see the potential for a better future, even when it's hard. I always tell my clients "It will never be the same, but it can always be better." You have to visualize a happy marriage. What does a happy marriage even look like? If you can't see it in your mind, how will you ever know when you have experienced it? Have faith in yourself and in your partner. Believe in your marriage! If you want it, you can have it, as long as you don't give up!

Finally, it's important to have **TRUST.** You have to trust your spouse when you take the risk to open your heart and try again. This can be so hard 1) because you don't want to forgive or 2) because you are taking a risk that your trust will be taken for granted or abused. Yes, this is difficult when you've been hurt or betrayed. But if you want the marriage to work, and your partner is genuinely sorry for their actions, trust is required. Don't get me wrong: trust should not just be given freely. It is proven by consistent action and honesty. It may take time, but it can't take forever if you want to move forward in your marriage. Trust gives you the opportunity to grow in your relationship.

Be Courageous
Fight for Your Marriage
It's worth it!

When you have courage, you are bold and determined. You can't fight if you're hiding behind fear, anger, or guilt or if you have no idea what you are fighting for. <u>Know what you are fighting for!</u> It should not **only** be for the kids, financial security, or "I just don't want to be alone." Fight for happiness. Fight for fulfillment. Fight for unconditional love. Set high standards for your marriage and reach for them. Work hard at restoring the broken places and healing the wounds. You have to be all in: both of you! It takes courage to dream again and go after what you both want, so fight for your marriage and expect positive results.

CHAPTER 3

COMMITMENT: How do we move forward?

Whe you break a bone, I've heard it is excruciatingly painful. Once it's broken, that pain doesn't just go away; the bone must be reset and given time to heal. Sometimes it's put in a cast or splint for extra support during the healing process. Marriage can be seen through a similar lens. When it lacks communication, affection, intimacy, or vitality, your marriage is broken. A broken marriage, just like a bone, usually needs time and support in order to heal.

Now when your marriage has been completely shattered (after an affair, death, financial crisis, etc.), this requires total replacement. Not in the sense that you get rid of your partner! But you will have to replace patterns of behavior, concepts, and/or beliefs. You may have to change your approach to your marriage. The old way of loving each other may not work anymore. This is when it's time to reevaluate.

You essentially have 3 options:

1. *change it,*
2. *accept it, or*
3. *let it go.*

Now I know I mentioned this earlier, but it's a point that I really want to bring home. There are events that you cannot change. If something is final, it happened, and there is no going back to where you were. This may be a situation where you have to accept what has happened. If you lost your job- can't change it. You have to accept it and MOVE FORWARD. If she had an affair and you want your marriage to work, you have to accept it, forgive, and MOVE FORWARD. If you lose someone close to you, you can't change it; it will never be the same. You have to accept it, cherish the good memories, and MOVE FORWARD. You see, in each situation, the goal is to develop forward thinking and not remain stuck in the past.

Change It, Accept It or Let it Go

For example: consider an affair. You are totally devastated, and you are unsure if your marriage can ever recover from the blow. Here are a few questions to ask:

1. **Can trust be restored?** Will you ever trust them again? Was their betrayal so painful that you can't move forward, or is this something painful but ultimately bearable? Ask yourself whether you and your partner can work through this.

2. **Can you forgive?** Forgiving doesn't mean you agree with your partner's decisions. It only means you will no longer hold on to anger, resentment, or bitterness toward your spouse and you free yourself from the clutches of the pain. When you free yourself, the past no longer controls your emotions: *you do.*

3. **Can you let go?** When you are holding onto a painful memory or experience, it is hard to enjoy new experiences. Think of your memory as a fist: if it's clenched, it can't receive. If it stays clenched too long, it starts to hurt. When you let go, you open yourself up again. When you let go of hurtful memories and experiences, you give your marriage another chance.

4. **Can you move forward?** Are you willing to let the past stay in the past, embrace the present, and create a new future? You have to develop new goals, desires, and aspirations. Moving forward means allowing the pain to drive you toward a better future. Can we take this experience and use it to grow? Rather than living in the past, can you work with the negative experience and create a new normal? Identify where things went wrong, address it proactively, and look forward to a brighter future.

These are huge steps toward recovery. As you go through this process, you may still feel vulnerable or weak. You take the risk of being hurt again, but we all know that life is risky, and you are taking a chance at reaching higher levels of fulfilment with your spouse. When you and your spouse have moved past the pain and become focused on the present moment, you can begin to create a better future. And for that reason, it may be worth the risk.

HOWEVER, if you answered "no" to any of the above questions, you probably need to consider whether staying in the marriage is worth it. There is no point in staying in a painful relationship or holding on to something that you know can never be repaired. If this is the case, you will move to the next step. If trust (#1) and forgiveness (#2) cannot be achieved, let it go (#3) so you can be free from the pain and move on with your life (#4). Whether you choose to stay or go, the ultimate goal is to move forward with your life instead of remaining trapped in the pain of the past.

Following betrayal, don't be surprised if your spouse questions things you do. This is just a part of the recovery process… Let them heal… Be honest and regain their trust

Here's a question: What should you do if you are the betrayer? A few things to consider:

- Acknowledge the hurt and pain you caused them ("I hurt you… I let you down… I was wrong.")
- Provide a sincere apology, and don't make promises you can't keep (saying "I'll never hurt you again" is not true. Hopefully you won't hurt them in the same capacity, but you always have the capability to let them down)
- Recognize that it will take time to heal (don't rush this process)
- Don't expect your spouse to move on right away (just because you've moved on doesn't mean that they have).
- Expect them to question your actions/decisions. They may ask a million times (who, what, when, why, where). You must be ready for that.

Considerations:

1. **NEVER think you are immune to betrayal- this is a fallacy.** Don't say "it could never happen to me," because broken trust can happen to anyone in any situation. It is important to realize that if you were in the betrayer's shoes, feeling what they felt at the moment, it could have been you! If you were unhappy in your marriage and the right person at the right time came into your life and showed you the love, attention and affection that you needed… who's to say you wouldn't slip into the same trap? I know that it's easy to say "I would NEVER do that." And maybe you won't, but that doesn't mean that you or your spouse are not capable of making a mistake

Don't fall in love with fantasy: you will always be hurt in the end...

2. **You may have inadvertently contributed to the problem**. Many times we blame our spouse for what they do, but we don't see how we could have contributed to the problem. This is not always the case, but if they try to explain WHY they did what they did, and you disregard what they say because you are hurt, you lose sight of why the incident occurred. When you accept the fact that you are not perfect, and you stop holding people to higher standards than yourself, you may have a little more empathy. You may show a little mercy or extend a little more grace in the situation.

Testimonial:

"I'll be the first to say I haven't been the perfect spouse nor will I ever be. I've disappointed my husband so many times. But I had to own it. I had to accept that I wasn't perfect and so did he. The illusion that "I would never hurt him" was just that- AN ILLUSION. Whether a major blow or a minor setback, you can comeback- if you choose. There is no rule that says you can't recover. It truly depends on how much is too much for you. Don't stay out of obligation. Stay because that's what you want...

3. **You must have realistic expectations.** First of all, don't fall in love with fantasy. You must always be realistic about the risk of disappointment. Sometimes, when you see the situation for what it is, you realize disappointment can happen to anyone. Furthermore, if you were aware of your partner's flaws when you met them, why would you expect anything different? If you were aware of how your partner interacted with others, why would you expect anything different with you? Now I'm not saying that people can't change, because many times they do. Bad habits can be changed, but your spouse has to want to change them. Your spouse must genuinely want to be and become a better spouse.

In the event that they don't want to change their behavior, then you may have to evaluate how you will respond.

4. **Once it's done, it's done. You can't change it, so you must move past it!** This may mean you forgive, or it may mean you decide to leave. I can't make that choice for you, but I can help you see the options for what they are. One thing to remember: Don't harbor resentment, because if you do, both of you will likely be miserable. And who wants to live like that?

5. **If you choose to forgive**, **don't hold it over their head.** So many times, we say "I forgive you," but we continue to bring it up over and over again. If you've truly forgiven, then it's over and in the past. However, if you continue to repeat the same story over and over, you should consider your motives. Are you trying to hurt your spouse for what they did to hurt you? Or are you still hurting due to unresolved issues? Either way, this has to stop if you want to move beyond the pain. Counseling is always a great option.

6. **What can you learn?** How can both of you grow from this experience?
   Many times, rebuilding trust makes the relationship stronger, but you have to be committed to the process. In other words, you make up your mind that you are in this together no matter what. It takes a strong couple to do this, and understand not everyone can. That's okay. Just know you are in for a bumpy ride when you are repairing your marriage.

Your marriage can be better, but you have to commit to making it happen. You can't just believe; you have to know. Start by evaluating your past, your present, and what could be the future. Give it time, be patient, and have realistic expectations when repairing a broken relationship. No matter how challenging it may seem, if you both work together, it's possible.

CHAPTER 4

ASPIRATION- Reach Higher, Grow Stronger

Strong relationships are based on deep friendships and emotional connections. They don't just happen, there is a process to creating the marriage you want. According to John Gottman, a relationship expert and founder of the Gottman Institute insist that part of the process of building a strong relationship is to support each other's aspirations. So what exactly does that mean?

ASPIRE- to have strong ambition or hope of achieving something

Aspiration can apply to goals in any area of your life. And in your marriage, aspirations keep you reaching toward higher levels of happiness and satisfaction. So if you aspire to have a strong, stable relationship, here are a few things to keep in mind:

Aim high

Don't settle for less than the best in your marriage. Don't get in the mundane routine saying "This is just how it is- I guess things will never change." NO NO NO! Don't accept that! Set specific and realistic goals that you can achieve easily. Both long-term and short-term goals are beneficial. Try to consider setting goals that would benefit your relationship. Now go for it!

Spend time dreaming

Think about the things you want to accomplish in your marriage. Maybe this is financial freedom, your dream vacation, or that beautiful new house. Visualize your future together, and start dreaming again!

Sit down and plan out how you can make these dreams a reality.

Prepare for the highs and lows

Life is full of challenges; you need to be ready to tackle and overcome them. Don't go into a fight expecting to lose. Don't play the game without trying to score. Don't just go through life existing: PLAN TO WIN! Plan for success, and if things don't go according to plan (and sometimes they don't), you know that you've given your all and put forth the effort. You worked hard, and you didn't give up. Next time, you will try harder with greater wisdom and insight than before! An awesome motivational speaker, Les Brown, "If you can look up, you can get up." Don't stay down. You can get up, and can climb higher than ever before.

Ignore the noise

Don't let someone else's negativity stand in the way of the marriage you want. Just because their relationship didn't work, that doesn't mean that yours won't. Fight for what you believe in. Fight for what you want. Let them watch, but don't accept their criticism as truth.

Repetition

REPEAT WHAT WORKS! You need ongoing progress- if it works, do it again! If it didn't work the first time, then improve it and move forward and don't quit. When you repeat what works, you're building momentum. Put in the work and expect positive results.

Excel

Reach for greater heights. Don't just go after your dreams: go beyond them. Don't stop growing and learning together. Things will change. likes, dislikes, personalities, and appearances. Whatever you aspire to, do it with excellence.

There are no limits to having a happy, healthy marriage. The possibilities are infinite. You just have to be open and receptive.

Important Factors to Maintaining a Strong Marriage:

- Stay focused on the strengths of your marriage, not the weaknesses.
- Every small progression leads you closer to fulfillment
- Build your friendship; this is the foundation of a healthy marriage.
- For every negative interaction, reset with 3-4 positive interactions. Cancel out the negative.
- Reinforce positive behaviors by expressing gratitude and appreciation. Always acknowledge it when things are done right.

If you can focus on building your marriage and not watching it fall apart, you can create enjoyable experiences. There is so much potential to be happy when you have the right tools. Don't expect to be happy if you are not striving for it. Lasting relationships need development, positive experiences, and awareness of the potential to be great. Aspire to have the marriage you want and achieve your dreams.

CHAPTER 5

REFLECTION- RESET and Push Forward

Sometimes, when things are going wrong, you have to push the "RESET BUTTON." Just like when your computer freezes or you're playing a video game and get stuck, RESET will take you back to the beginning and let you start over. Eric and I have started over many times over the years. Sometimes, it was due to unexpected blows, and other times it was due to inconsiderate actions that resulted in negative consequences. Rather than giving up, it's better to just RESET and start over again.

It's important to realize relationships have different levels. As you progress through these levels, it sometimes becomes more difficult to get to the next. Each level of your relationship will bring bigger challenges, and more advanced skills will always be required to overcome the obstacles. RESET give you the opportunity to start over and get things right.

Maybe you messed up and have to start over again. Maybe you said the wrong thing, made a huge mistake, or just got off-course. Learn to RESET!

EXAMPLE:

You haven't been out together in years. You don't even talk anymore. You are always in different rooms- one lounging on the couch while the other is upstairs, scrolling on social media. There is a terrible disconnect between you, and you don't know where it started. This is a great opportunity to RESET. Recognize the problem, talk about it, and develop a plan of action.

1) We don't spend time together
2) What should we do?
3) Develop and implement a plan

Instead of lounging and scrolling, try taking time to do something together. Cook dinner together, go for a walk, or share an ice cream sundae. You have to start somewhere! And remember, it's always important to take action.

Here is the process to RESET:

R- *Remember why you fell in love*

This is a huge part of the process of resetting your marriage. If you can't remember what brought you together, then how can you establish a foundation to build on when you are trying to repair your marriage?

TIP: Try to remember what being in love felt like. Think back to sweet moments in your relationship.

Always
have an
Attitude of Gratitude

E- *Express to your partner why they are important to you*

Gratitude is so important. Be thankful for your spouse; they are in your life for a reason. Remind them that your marriage is important and so are they. Let them know that you value them even though your marriage is in a tough spot. Recognize that it's just time to reconnect again.

TIP: Don't devalue your partner with your words. No one wants to feel inferior or inadequate. Build their self-esteem and their confidence in the marriage. Tell them when they do things you appreciate; don't just expect them to know!

S- *Spend time together. Spark interest: do things you used to do that made you happy*

Start doing things together again. What are things that you used to do that brought joy to your relationship? When you were dating, where did you go? What did you like? You can also try doing new things and developing new hobbies.

TIP: Do something special together at least twice a month. Weekly would be great, but if you're married with kids, twice a month is reasonable.

Action Always Results in Reaction.
Your behavior affects their response…

E- *Engage in loving actions. Do things they want to do (activities), don't be selfish (focusing only on what you want out of the marriage), show them how much you care, and take time for intimacy*

Okay, so this one is hard. If you're not doing well in your marriage, the last thing you want to do is "show love". But it doesn't have to be over the top. Maybe you can buy his favorite snack when you're at the store, or you can watch her favorite movie. Take time to engage in loving actions instead of just saying empty words.

For men, connecting with your wife increases the likelihood of intimacy. One of the best ways to connect to her is through communication. LISTEN to her. For women, when you haven't talked or shared ideas with one another, it's hard to become or stay intimate. Most women don't want intimacy without some form of communication. (Remember, men, share your thoughts and feelings as well).

One of the best ways for women to show love to their husbands is by giving support. Many times, women complain about what men are not doing. Try saying something positive first, instead of dumping emotional frustration. Giving him quality time without complaint or "nagging" can also be affirming to your husband as well. Ultimately, the most important thing is to SHOW your spouse you love them, not just say it. Find out your spouse's love language (research Gary Chapman's "5 Love Languages"), and get to work! Once you connect on these levels, you will likely see a drastic change in your marriage dynamic.

T- *Take time to explore new things*

TIP: Maybe you'll decide to go horseback riding for the first time, or you've always wanted to see the Grand Canyon. Find things that they've always wanted to do, and do them. Start planning; even though you may not want to do it, this is an opportunity for change. If you want something different, you have to do something different. Go on a picnic. Join a gym. Go to the movies. Learn how to Salsa: anything to get you going.

Over time, your marriage may feel old and stagnant. You have to RESET to get back to a place of enjoyment. Happy couples work hard at maintaining their relationship. It doesn't just happen. When things get challenging, talk about it, RESET, and work on moving forward without holding on to the past. "Why didn't you" or "You never" is not going to help you RESET. Be positive, stay focused, and expect positive results.

CHAPTER 6

INTENTION– Develop A Plan and Work It

Your marriage needs a blueprint, which is a plan you follow that keeps you on track. You should do this early in your marriage, but even in a mature marriage you can evaluate progress or add goals along the way. As a couple, you should look into your future, develop a plan, and design the marriage you want. Start initiating the process of change *now*. Build on your strengths. It's not just an individual responsibility; it takes both of you building together.

Consider that one of you may be better at managing the bills. The other may be great at organizing or scheduling. Regardless of who is better at what, take these strengths and use them to your advantage. It takes both of you! Be focused on working together to reach your goals no matter what.

Here are a few things you should have in your marriage blueprint:

<u>Vision</u>
What you intend to accomplish

<u>Mission Statement</u>
What your relationship stands for

<u>Goals And Objectives</u>
Necessary steps to
accomplish your goals

#1- Establish your Values:
What's important to you? Identify your highest priorities and keep them in mind as you identify your goals.

Example:

Family, leisure, money, career, health, spirituality

#2- Establish your Vision & Mission:

This should be concise, specific, realistic, ambitious, and aligned with your values.

Example:

Our Vision: To experience the best in our marriage and reach fulfillment together.

Our Mission: We will build a solid foundation to establish a home filled with peace, love, and joy through our commitment to each other.

#3- Establish your Goals & Objectives:

From this point, every goal you develop should align with your values and mission. How do you know you've accomplished something without having a goal to work toward? You should determine what happiness and fulfillment look like for you. Success is measurable; it is determined by your progress toward your goals. Accomplishing these goals gives you something to be excited about, and that gives you momentum.

EXAMPLES:

We will keep God first in our lives.

- Pray together daily
- Attend church on Sundays to maintain our faith.

We will always value each other's opinion, even if we don't disagree.

- Work on our communication skills by using "I" statements
- Always resolve conflict within 24 hours
- Always be respectful no matter how angry we become

We will maintain a healthy balance in our lives

- Eat healthy meals
- Exercise daily

#4- Make decisions using your blueprint:

When making decisions, always make sure you consider what is best for your marriage. You have to communicate openly and honestly. You should also have a weekly or monthly "check-up" to monitor your progress.

Go to <u>www.FlipMyMarriage.com</u> for more great resources!

#5- Develop Your Relationship- You have to work for it!

Remember to grow individually and together. You should not focus all your attention on your marriage without also paying attention to yourself. This is not healthy. Personal development is just as important as relationship development, so you have to find a healthy balance. Working on yourself keeps your focus on personal happiness, which greatly contributes to the marriage.

Also, be sure to reinforce your spouse. You shouldn't only focus on what they are doing wrong, but focus on what they are doing right. Praise can go a long way. If you want them to continue doing something, make sure they know you appreciate it. Also make sure to follow-up with positive action, as love is displayed is oftentimes better than through words.

Finally, write your vision down. Put it on the refrigerator or mirror to remind you of what you are trying to accomplish in your marriage. Everyone wants to have a great marriage, but few are willing to do what it takes to have it.

CHAPTER 7

EMPOWERMENT: Be Strong & Confident

You have power and authority over your marriage. Do you believe that? Well, it's true. Many of the outcomes we face are simply the consequences of our own actions. As a couple- it's important to understand that your decisions today affect everything tomorrow. As you make healthy decisions- have a positive attitude- express love daily- pay attention to details- pray together

Believe in Yourself

Sometimes you have to reinforce that you are a good person and you deserve to be treated as such; if the one you love happens to be the one bringing you down- you need to evaluate your relationship and have a discussion about what you need to feel supported

Be Confident

Be confident in your personal power to be happy; feel good about yourself and your relationship; **Your relationship should enhance your life**; You should feel empowered by your partnership- the support, love and security that you feel because you are together- "He/ She has my back"

Positive Attitude

Attitude is EVERYTHING- if you feel good about your relationship- your behavior typically reflects that; the way you see yourself and the way you see your partner definitely matters in your relationship; see the good in your partner and reinforce when they do things right

Take Responsibility

OWN your relationship- recognize your part in your circumstance- it's not always their fault- sometimes we both contribute to the problems we face- work together to find solutions

Take Action

Set goals for the relationship and accomplish them- start small to gain momentum; this is a great way to build confidence in your relationship and in yourself

Create Your Environment

Take pride in what you have and what you do; it's YOUR job to make the best of whatever situation you choose to be in; take the initiative to set the atmosphere in your home and set the tone of your day – create a healthy environment for yourself

Make a Commitment

Make the commitment to be "all in"; when you are committed-you give effort, take risks and make sacrifices- basically IT TAKES WORK; Commit to giving your best and take the time to figure out what will make your relationship successful.

CONCLUSION

Work hard to gain the things you want out of life. Don't allow life to happen *to* you; make it happen *for* you. It's up to you, because you always have a choice to be happy. You don't have to be miserable. There is always something you can do differently. I encourage everyone reading this to consider what's most important to you, and whether you want to say "I'm married" or "I'm *happily* married." No one should just be married without getting any fulfillment out of it. Invest in your marriage, and plan your marriage. Set goals, create opportunities to enjoy each other, and remember what brought you together. IT'S POSSIBLE to have a good marriage, but it's all up to you!

ATTACHMENTS

Flip My Marriage
"7 Keys to Enhance Your Relationship"

Definition of VISION

: a thought, concept or object formed in the imagination

What is your VISION for this relationship?

1 year from now

1)_____(HIS)

2)_____(HERS)

3)_____(BOTH)

5 years from now

1)_____(HIS)

2)_____(HERS)

3)_____(BOTH)

10 years from now

1)_____(HIS)

2)_____(HERS)

3)_____(BOTH)

Value Systems:

What are your VALUES (what's most important to you)?

HIS   HERS

_____   _____

_____   _____

_____   _____

_____   _____

KEY #1: BE GOAL-ORIENTED

Question: How will we get to where we want to be in life? Set Goals!

Goal 1)

_____

Goal 2)

_____

Goal 3)

_____

Specific_____ Measurable_____ Achievable_____ Realistic_____ Timely_____

What wakes you up in the morning?

Goals+Plans=Success

What drives you?

What are you passionate about?

Don't be afraid to dream. Reignite your <u>PASSION</u> for life!

"Most people fail in life not because they aim too high and miss, but because they aim too low and hit."

-LES BROWN, Motivational Speaker

"What would you

dare to dream

if you knew

you could **NOT FAIL?**"

-BRIAN TRACY, Motivational Speaker

FEAR OF FAILURE

False **E**vidence **A**ppearing **R**eal

    False **E**valuation of **A**ctual **R**eality

        Fallacy **E**xperienced **A**s **R**eal

nEGatiVE THinKiNg- Stunts your growth

What if she leaves me? What if he doesn't love me anymore? What if we lose everything? Why does this always happen to me? Will I ever be happy? Will I ever get ahead?

Question: What negative thoughts keep you from growing? (Be honest!).

HIS

1) _____

2) _____

3) _____

HERS

1) _____

2) _____

3) _____

KEY #2: FOCUS ON THE PRESENT

"What you FOCUS on becomes your REALITY. Don't focus on the past- LEARN FROM IT. Don't worry about the future- CREATE IT. Focus on the present. FOCUS ON THE HERE AND NOW. This moment is all you have. Every second that passes is a missed OPPORTUNITY."
-Christina Hopson-Allen, LPC

Question: What events from the past are hindering you from positively experiencing your present?

Question: What can you do TODAY to have a more fulfilling relationship?

(HINT: What has your partner been nagging you to do??? Wash the car? Save money?)

HIS

1) _____

2) _____

3) _____

HERS

1) _____

2) _____

3) _____

FORGIVENESS- It's not for them, it's for YOU!!

Question: Are there things you need to forgive him/her for that you are still holding on to?

3 Options: CHANGE IT – ACCEPT IT – LET LET IT GO!!!

We have to learn to move FORWARD.

KEY #3: BE SOLUTION-FOCUSED

Focus on the solution NOT the problem.

Look for alternatives.

Make a decision.

Be determined.

Question: What problems do you face? What are options to solve the problem? Make a decision on how to solve the issue. If it doesn't work, re-evaluate. Try, then try AGAIN!

BIGGEST PROBLEM THAT YOU ARE CURRENTLY FACING:

_____

_____

Alternatives to solving the problem:

1) _____

2) _____

KEY #4: SHOW COMPASSION & UNDERSTANDING

- Understand Your Partner's Perspective
- Acknowledge His/Her Needs
- Importance of Validation

Empathy, Sympathy, Acknowledgment, Validation, Understanding

Effective Communication: You can't just listen to what they say, but you have to understand what they mean!

Learn to use "I" statements: I feel _____ when you _____

Always reflect what you think they are saying:

"I here you saying that _____. Is this true?"

10 TIPS FOR EFFECTIVE COMMUNICATION

1. Stop & Listen- Learn when to HUSH!
2. Hear what they mean, not just want they say
3. Openness & honesty is key
4. Look for clues- pay attention to nonverbal cues
5. Stay focused in the moment- the here & now
6. Self-control is important- Your response is not always required
7. The ability to compromise will come in handy
8. Laughter helps breaks down walls
9. Communication is dialogue not just "talk"
10. Gain insight and understanding

KEY #6: EXPRESS APPRECIATION

Do you ever tell him/her what they are doing right?
Or do you ALWAYS focus on the negative?

Give your partner 5 reasons that you appreciate them:

HIS   HERS

_____   _____

_____   _____

_____   _____

_____   _____

_____   _____

KEY #7: DEVELOP A SOLID FOUNDATION

We will ALWAYS:

1) _____

2) _____

3) _____

<u>Get the Tools, Do the Work, Flip Your Marriage TODAY!!!</u>

<u>10 Keys to A Successful Relationship</u>

1. **TRUST**

You have to trust in a marriage. And when I say this, I mean having assurance and confidence in one's intentions. Trust in your partner is believing that they want the best for the relationship and that they are giving every effort to make it work. Trust is really essential in building the foundation of a marriage. Having doubt only causes stress on the relationship and causes excessive worry. Without trust, you can't fully enjoy your marriage because you are always skeptical, suspicious or expecting the worst.

Now for some of you, trust may be difficult. Knowing that it is a prerequisite for a happy marriage may be unfortunate because they haven't always been trustworthy in the past. Maybe there has been hurt or one of you fell short of the expectation as a spouse. But if you want to be fulfilled in your marriage, there must be trust. And after the pain of disappointment- trust may not be something that is freely given, but earned by consistent action over time. Once there has been distrust, it has to be earned back by providing sufficient evidence (proof) that you are trustworthy.

Trust builds courage, strength, and confidence. Be trustworthy and do what you say you're going to do. Let them know they can depend on you!

2. **COMMUNICATION**

You have to learn to listen. You can't just hear what they say, but you have to understand what they mean. For example- "You're never at home" may actually mean "I miss you and I wish we could spend more time together." Now it would be great if they would just SAY THAT! But we all know that this is not always the case.

It's really hard for someone to "read between the lines" so here are a few things to consider:

- Tone of voice is very important- when they raise their voice means they are really trying to get a point across- there is intense emotions behind what it said- it may even come to the point of being disrespectful

- Take note of body language- rolling eyes, smirking, crossed arms, etc.
- Learn to be assertive- express what you feel without being aggressive (trying to make them hear you) or being too passive (not wanting to hurt their feelings).
- Be clear, concise and direct.
- Learn how to talk it out- sit down at the kitchen table and talk about the finances, the kids, retirement- whatever is important to your relationship.
- Be respectful- don't talk over them or make them feel like you don't care. And even if you don't care- make effort to support them by saying "Wow, sorry you feel that way" or "that must really be tough" or "I understand what you are saying"
- Know that your feelings matter as well- express what you feel and try to find middle ground (compromise)
- Actively listen to what they have to say and ask for clarification if you don't understand- DON'T ASSUME- we all know what that means!

3. COMMITMENT

Your commitment is necessary to make the relationship work. You can't be half in and half out- either you're ALL IN or you're just wasting time. Commitment is a requirement for a fulfilling relationship. And if you find yourself questioning your commitment- this needs to be addressed. Why do I feel this way? What happened that caused me to lose faith in my marriage? What can we do to restore our promise to love and cherish each other? You both must be dedicated to celebrating the good times and enduring the bad. Learn to hold on to one another when it's tough and lift each other up when you want to give up. Set goals, talk about your dreams, establish your values and find purpose in your relationship- always have something to look forward to. Remember: **It takes TEAMWORK**! And make sure you always make your marriage a priority- otherwise you will look back and find that somewhere along the way you disconnected.

4. STABILITY

Your overall stability is important for a successful marriage. Emotional, relational and financial stability- these three factors will make or break you. Finding balance by learning the process of give and take can help you develop stability. Understand that a stable marriage is a happy marriage- It means everyone's needs are being met and no one feels depleted. I always talk about the "love box" with couples. It's like a small box between you- You both put in, you both pull out. The key is that you have to put things in that your partner actually wants and vice versa. If you put in affirmation and they don't respond to that, it will get left in the box. So when they go to pull something out- there isn't anything that will fulfill their need- YOU PUT THE WRONG THING IN THE BOX (maybe they actually needed physical affection instead)! Or if they buy gifts but all you really want is quality time, this could be a problem down the road (you don't want them buying your love but showing their love). There are several needs that are important in a relationship (you can even check out the "5 Love Languages" by Gary Chapman online and take a quick quiz to find out what your needs are). When you give your spouse what they need (timing also plays a part in this as well), they are more likely to give back to you. The important thing is that you both **KNOW WHAT YOUR NEEDS ARE**! Learn to give them what they need and expect to receive just as much in return- _but you have to understand the process (the love box)_. Once the cycle of giving and receiving starts, you can continuously keep it going which brings a state of equilibrium to your marriage.

5. **FAITH**

Your faith will keep you committed. Your faith will keep you focused. Your faith will keep you grounded. It will keep you from giving up and walking away. It will keep your sanity when the marriage appears to be falling apart and you feel like you're losing your mind. If you both have the expectation that your commitment to the marriage will pay off, it will. But you have to BELIEVE THAT IT'S POSSIBLE to be truly happy in your marriage. Trust that you can overcome any obstacle together. The key is that you are TOGETHER. Now, it's possible that you can have faith in your spouse. I've seen this work many times. But God is usually in the midst of this. When you are both committed to God, your faith can truly work miracles- but your partner has to be open and want change as well. If they have given up, then this will be a more difficult challenge- this is a common situation that opens the door to divorce. But if there is the smallest glimmer of faith- IT'S POSSIBLE...

6. **PATIENCE**

Your patience in the process of building a successful marriage is required. It's part of the package when you say "I DO." So many times we think that we "become one" at the altar, but this is not the case. You become "one" with priority (putting your partner first), perseverance, and priority. You make the choice, but then you have to allow the process of "becoming one" to occur. You should allow them room to grow and make mistakes. Understand that having a mature relationship takes time- it's a process. You have to be patient and offer support to one another. With patience comes forgiveness- with patience comes tolerance- with patience comes fortitude- with patience comes reward.

7. ACCEPTANCE

No one is perfect. You must be willing to accept the good with the bad- flaws and all. There is a level of grace required- understanding that they are human and will make mistakes. In addition, you must also identify your strengths and learn to balance one another. One of you may be better at managing the money- the other may be better at managing the kids busy schedule. Learn to use your strengths as an advantage. At the same time, learn to acknowledge your weakness and work to improve them. It's important to understand your spouse's weaknesses and learn to balance with your own strengths. Accept them for who they are and allow them to grow.

8. CHEMISTRY

Attraction is a key component of any relationship. There should be some level of chemistry for your marriage to work- not just sexual but on a more intimate level. Focus on what you love about them- the things that attracted you to them in the beginning. Also consider the things that you have grown to love over time. Desire your partner for their inner beauty as well as outward. Don't bank on outward physical appearance to keep you in love, but seek characteristics about them that make you want them more. Focus on your friendship and increase intimacy through communication and emotional connection.

9. UNCONDITIONAL LOVE

Unconditional love is kind and gentle- it is compassionate and empathetic- it gives and doesn't take. Unconditional love means you love them despite their flaws. You love them, through their mistakes. You accept them for who they are and offer them support when they need it most. When you love unconditionally, you are not judgmental but open and forgiving. This is the greatest love you can experience.

10. **INSPIRATION**

In a relationship, you should be inspired to grow and "do better." You can't just settle for less. You have to be willing to learn more about the dynamics of your relationship. Study your partner and gain knowledge about their goals and aspirations. Motivate them to be the best they can be. Recognize their potential and help them reach their goals. You will find that when your partner is happy, you may be a little happier too!

Printed in the United States
by Baker & Taylor Publisher Services